METZ CATHEDRAL

Texte by

Marie-Isabelle Soupart
&
Philippe Hiegel

Translated by
Ray Beaumont-Craggs

The portal of the Virgin.

INTRODUCTION

It would seem that never before have the cathedrals of France been visited by so many people who do not know the origin or purpose of such an edifice.

By definition, a cathedral is the main church of a bishop's see, containing the cathedra or episcopal throne; Metz cathedral claims to possess the throne of its founder and first bishop, Saint Clement, circa 280. Very often it is also the mother-church which gave rise to the city's other churches. In Paris, the first churches admitted to the status of parish were considered to be the subsidiaries of Notre-Dame, and until the Revolution the expression "*the daughters of Notre-Dame*" was used to designate the oldest among them.

In the Middle Ages, the cathedral was truly a city within the city. The cathedral also included the bishop's house which he shared with his clergy, because the development of parishes both within and without the city walls did not prevent the bishop from retaining near him a certain number of priests, deacons and other clerics to assist him in the administration of the diocese as well as with the cathedral liturgy. That is the origin of the chapter of canons in the service of the cathedral to whom, at Metz, the great bishop Saint Chrodegang (742-766) gave a Rule in about 755 A.D.

The wealth of the chapter, the foundations, private devotions, the development of cathedral liturgy, all resulted in a complex multitude of constructions set around the cathedral. So it is that at Metz, around Saint-Etienne, the great church includes several small ones: Saint John the Baptist (the baptistry), Notre-Dame-la-Ronde, Saint-Pierre-le-Majeur, Saint-Pierre-le-Vieux, Saint-Paul, Sainte-Galle (the episcopal oratory), the cloister, the schools, a tower, the episcopal palace...

Until the Revolution, the chapter's main function was to provide the means of support for the religious cult together with everyday and exceptional upkeep of the edifice. After the Concordat, cathedrals became the property of the State, which replaced the chapter for a major part of the upkeep and alterations to the building, but very often, as was the case at Strasbourg and Metz, the cathedral Œuvre (foundation) inherited some of the chapter's time-honoured responsibility, usually with very limited means.

House of God and house of the people of God, the cathedral vibrates in harmony with all the great events of the bishopric and the city: ordination and funeral of the bishop, ordination of priests and deacons, diocesan assemblies, *Te Deums* and patriotic ceremonies...

On the 10th of October 1988, Metz cathedral was honoured by a visit of Pope John-Paul II when he came to Alsace-Lorraine. Each year, in the entire diocese, the anniversary of the cathedral's dedication is celebrated in order to commemorate the end of its construction, or at least of the major structure, and the consecration of the edifice to God. Metz cathedral was consecrated on the 27th of June 1039.

The candles burning near Notre-Dame de bon-Secours bear witness to the prayers of many unknown pilgrims, while the canonical liturgy, although very reduced today in comparison with what it once was, ensures daily divine worship. On major feast-days, the bishop officiates pontifically.

At Metz, as elsewhere, the cathedral and the city are linked by a history spanning the centuries. The Mutte tower, for example, is the town belfry. Its bell's peal rang out for the last time to mark the 1918 Armistice; it now chimes daily the twelve strokes of noon and every quarter hour on election days.

Therefore it is no exaggeration to say that the cathedral is the very soul of the city, today's city which goes there to express its aspirations, its anxieties and its prayers, as did yesterday's. As Cardinal Pacelli declared at Paris Notre-Dame cathedral on the 13th of July 1937 in his speech on the vocation of France, in the heart of the city, the cathedral is *"an Orate Fratres in stone, a perpetual invitation to prayer"*

fr. Pierre RAFFIN, o.p.
bishop of Metz

For further information,
read **La cathédrale aujourd'hui**, sous la direction du ministère de la Culture et du Centre National de Pastorale liturgique, Editions Desclée, 1992.

FOREWORD

A guide-book is difficult to write: it must enumerate all that one sees and explain it briefly. It is practical during a visit, but when it is read at home afterwards it soon becomes tedious due to the abundance of detail and to certain types of description which are constantly repeated.

This guide-book makes it clear that it is not possible to separate the cathedral from its history. The Hun invasion of 451 A.D. is the reason that it was built on an emplacement so obviously unsuitable for the construction of a vast monument.

The brilliant idea which inspired the authorities of the cathedral and of Notre-Dame-la-Ronde to rebuild their churches under one roof resulted in some important factors: the placing of the towers and portals, spacious windows on the west front opening onto the present-day cathedral square.

These various elements brought an originality of style very different from that of a typical cathedral. But the features which made it attractive disconcerted certain people whose ideal seemed to be that our cathedral should become ordinary. The towers could not be moved, but the lower section of the stained-glass windows on the west facade was eliminated in order to create a portal. Metz roofs are very low, those of the cathedral were raised, which overwhelmed the towers. Engravings of the cathedral as it was before the 1878 fire show how much of their elegance the towers have lost.

Certain characteristics are recognised by everyone, notably the elegance of the great nave whose height astounds the unprepared visitor, the area of glass which makes it a veritable museum of the art of stained-glass and of its evolution.

Although the sculpture cannot be compared to that of Chartres or of Rheims, it is not without merit and this guide-book notes some interesting details.

May this booklet help you to benefit from your visit.

Abbot André Dukiel
President of the cathedral Foundation

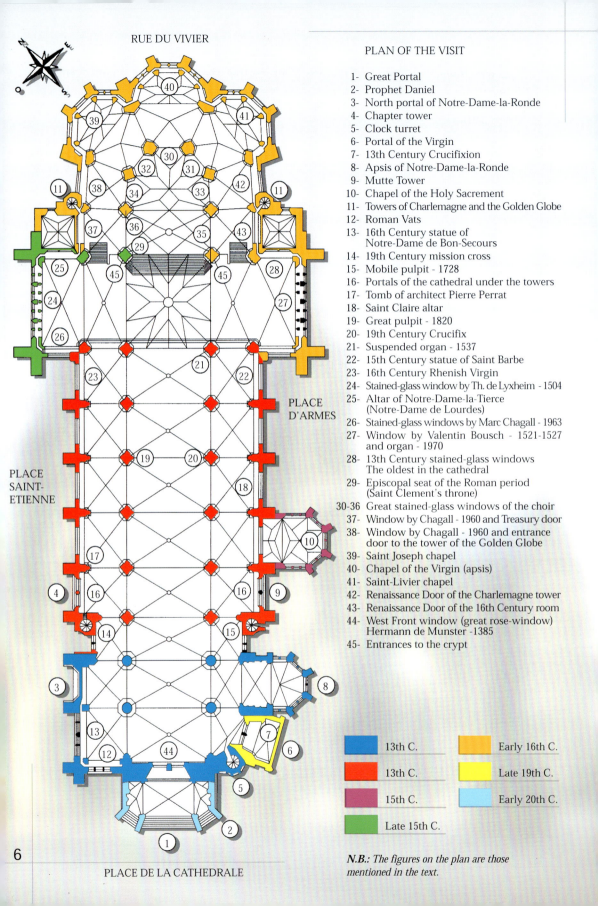

RUE DU VIVIER

PLAN OF THE VISIT

1- Great Portal
2- Prophet Daniel
3- North portal of Notre-Dame-la-Ronde
4- Chapter tower
5- Clock turret
6- Portal of the Virgin
7- 13th Century Crucifixion
8- Apsis of Notre-Dame-la-Ronde
9- Mutte Tower
10- Chapel of the Holy Sacrement
11- Towers of Charlemagne and the Golden Globe
12- Roman Vats
13- 16th Century statue of
    Notre-Dame de Bon-Secours
14- 19th Century mission cross
15- Mobile pulpit - 1728
16- Portals of the cathedral under the towers
17- Tomb of architect Pierre Perrat
18- Saint Claire altar
19- Great pulpit - 1820
20- 19th Century Crucifix
21- Suspended organ - 1537
22- 15th Century statue of Saint Barbe
23- 16th Century Rhenish Virgin
24- Stained-glass window by Th. de Lyxheim - 1504
25- Altar of Notre-Dame-la-Tierce
    (Notre-Dame de Lourdes)
26- Stained-glass windows by Marc Chagall - 1963
27- Window by Valentin Bousch - 1521-1527
    and organ - 1970
28- 13th Century stained-glass windows
    The oldest in the cathedral
29- Episcopal seat of the Roman period
    (Saint Clement's throne)
30-36 Great stained-glass windows of the choir
37- Window by Chagall - 1960 and Treasury door
38- Window by Chagall - 1960 and entrance
    door to the tower of the Golden Globe
39- Saint Joseph chapel
40- Chapel of the Virgin (apsis)
41- Saint-Livier chapel
42- Renaissance Door of the Charlemagne tower
43- Renaissance Door of the 16th Century room
44- West Front window (great rose-window)
    Hermann de Munster -1385
45- Entrances to the crypt

PLACE
D'ARMES

PLACE
SAINT-
ETIENNE

	13th C.		Early 16th C.
	13th C.		Late 19th C.
	15th C.		Early 20th C.
	Late 15th C.		

PLACE DE LA CATHEDRALE

6

N.B.: The figures on the plan are those
mentioned in the text.

HISTORICAL BACKGROUND

It was towards the end of the 3rd Century that the first bishop, Saint Clement, arrived in Metz. He settled in the southern suburb, where stood the ruins of an enormous amphitheatre, near the present-day goods station. Clement founded a modest sanctuary, Metz's first cathedral.

The saint's successors continued his work. New sanctuaries appeared, outside and inside the town. In about 415 A.D. in the heart of the city, between the thermal baths and the Moselle, a solid basilica, Saint-Etienne oratory* was built on the emplacement of the actual cathedral, on land very steep to the north and east bounded by an angle of the city walls.

What was this oratory's origin? One can presume that it was fairly recent, because the cult of Saint Etienne (Saint Stephen) only became important in the West after the discovery of his relics, accompanied by great miracles. This event created, in 415 A.D., in Jerusalem and in the whole world, ardent devotion to the first martyr.

On Easter saturday of the year 451, Attila's hordes destroyed Metz in a fiery blood-bath. Only Saint-Etienne oratory survived the disaster with those inhabitants who had taken refuge in it. By the following century, Metz was re-born from its ruins; Saint-Etienne became the cathedral. It witnessed the pomp of the Austrasian court; the pontifical services of Arnoul (611-617) ancestor of the Carolingians; of Chrodegang (742-766) past minister to Pépin-le-Bref; of archbishop Drogon (823-855) son of Charlemagne. Saint Chrodegang, who introduced the Roman liturgy to Gaul and imposed communal life on his canons by virtue of a Rule gradually accepted by all the Church, beautified and enriched the edifice. With the backing of King Pépin, he built the altar, arcades around the choir and chancels fragments of which, found in 1914 during diggings in the cathedral choir, can still be seen today in the crypt. From this period, Saint-Etienne cathedral was surrounded by a number of religious buildings: the bishop's house, Saint-Pierre-le-Majeur, Notre-Dame, and a cloister which joined the churches together and which no doubt was already on the emplacement where it stood until the 18th Century (the present-day Place d'Armes).

Among the great feast-days that took place in this cathedral were the re-establishment of Louis-le-Débonnaire on the imperial throne in 835 and the coronation of Charles-le-Chauve as king of Lotharingia in 869. The venerable monument in which the crowning took place had entirely disappeared by the end of the 10th Century.

The reigns of the Ottonians and the Capetians, the reforms of Cluny and Gorze brought about a vast renewal of the arts. Metz took a determined part in this movement and replaced its decaying ancient church which was falling into ruin by a Romanesque cathedral similar to those in the valleys of the Meuse and the Rhine. Its construction was decided by bishop Thierry 1er (965-984) who was assisted by Emperor Otton 1er and his son Otton II. His successor Thierry II (1006-1047) was able to dedicate the new cathedral on the 27th of June 1040. Its foundations were discovered in 1914. The edifice had three naves, a transept and three apses. The nave was covered by visible woodwork. The choir occupied the square of the transept, framed by four tall pillars supporting great arcades. The central apse was flanked by two towers 41 metres in height, known as the Charlemagne towers. The main tower was situated on the west front.

The pre-Romanesque cathedral survived barely two centuries. Already, in the workshops of the Ile-de-France and of Champagne, a new style, which became known as Gothic, was being developed. Very soon it would dominate the whole of Christianity.

*It was not necessarily, as one understands it today, a small room for private worship. Etymologically speaking, an oratory is a place for prayer. The oldest historic document referring to a sanctuary is a passage in the **"History of the Franks"** by Grégoire de Tours (†594) in which the author gives this name to both small and big churches, so the Saint-Etienne oratory could have been either large or small.

Metz, in full economic and political progression, felt obliged to replace its small and deteriorating Romanesque cathedral by a vast and sumptuous building.

During the bishopric of Conrad de Scharfeneck (1212-1224), shortly after 1200 A.D., with the approval of the chapter, the construction of the cathedral began. However the exiguity and the unusual configuration of the terrain seemed an insurmountable problem. The downward slope towards the north and east (Place de Chambre and rue du Vivier) necessitated excessively costly substructures, and towards the south (Place d'Armes) the cloister and several adjoining sanctuaries made any extension impossible. There remained the west side, that of the façade, where stood the collegiate church of six canons called Notre-Dame-la-Rotonde (of the rotunda) or simply Notre-Dame-la-Ronde (the round) because of the circular shape of its apsis.

Enlarging the building obliged the sixty canons of the cathedral and those of the collegiate church to unite the two churches under the same roof. And that is what they did: Notre-Dame-la-Ronde formed the three final bays of the nave. However the level of its floor long remained above that of the cathedral. It is still possible today to distinguish the two churches by the four round pillars with no base remaining from Notre-Dame-la-Ronde.

The cathedral entrance was at the sides, by doors under the towers, and that of Notre-Dame-la-Ronde by the portal of the Virgin and another portal opening onto the Place de Chambre. At this period it was not yet possible to create a portal in the axis, because the west front of the church faced the courtyard of the bishop's palace.

In about 1350, bishop Adémar de Monteil (1327-1361) added the bishops' chapel, now the chapel of the Holy Sacrement, which was only completed in 1443 in the bishopric of Conrad Bayer de Boppart (1415-1459) by Jean de Commercy.

Construction of the main walls of the naves lasted around a hundred years, from the middle of the 13th Century to the middle of the 14th.

After a sixty-six year interruption, work began again. The vaulting of the upper nave was completed in 1380, at which time the wall separating Notre-Dame-la-Ronde and the cathedral was pulled down. The name of Pierre Perrat, master builder of the cathedral construction, appears for the first time in the chapter records: on the 7th of January 1386 he was given right of burial in the cathedral, a favour doubtless justified by important works such as the completion of the nave. He died in 1400.

The lofty, slender nave contrasted with the transept and the Romanesque choir. In 1486, Jacques d'Insming, vicar-general, canon and archdeacon of Metz, proposed to remodel at his expense the northern arm of the transept in which is the chapel of Notre-Dame-la-Tierce or Notre-Dame-l'Allemande. In 1487 he laid the foundation stone of this chapel. In 1503 began the demolition of the old choir, the Saint-Nicolas chapel in the southern arm, and the Charlemagne tower. Building took place at great speed and by the 11th of April 1522 it was possible to hold the solemn inauguration of the choir and the transept. The architecture of these parts reflects the decadence of the Gothic style, nevertheless the whole ensemble is subordinated to the original plan and nothing disturbs the interior's carefully organised harmony. Once again the difficult layout of the terrain, steeply sloping to the east, necessitated an unusual plan as it had done for the facade. Instead of an elongated choir, slightly raised, a large crypt had to be constructed to support a shortened but very elevated choir, with only three shallow chapels around the apse.

The cathedral was complete. Three long centuries of persistent effort had been nee- ded to bring this gigantic edifice to its conclusion.

9

Ancient Notre-Dame-la-Ronde nave.

No important alterations took place before the middle of the 18th Century. Since 1727 the governor of the bishopric province was the marshal of Belle-lsle, Fouquet's grandson. In 1754, despite protests from the chapter, he had the area surrounding the cathedral opened out by pulling down the cloister and the adjoining churches in order to create a square in honour of the king.

This series of monuments was no longer in fashion nor, it would seem, to the taste of marshal de Belle-lsle, who decided to eliminate them. But then wearied by the endless criticism aimed at him, he stopped the work, and when he died in 1761 the new Place d'Armes was unfinished.

In that same year arrived in Metz Jacques Francois Blondel, a parisian architect who drew up a general plan of redecoration. In 1764, he overlaid the west front with a classical portal which eliminated the lower section of the 14th Century stained-glass. The work was completed in the summer of 1766. The building of the great portal resulted in two alterations: the demolition of the corner portal of Notre-Dame, and the closure of the one opening onto the Place de Chambre.

Then it was decided to hide the base of the cathedral on its south side by constructing arcades identical to those of the groundfloor of the Town Hall. They were built from 1766 to 1769.

During the Revolution, the cathedral was subjected to considerable vandalism: from 1791 to 1793 nearly all the altars and tombs were destroyed. There was even a project to remove the stained-glass windows, but it was abandoned because it would have been too expensive. In 1795, a poster announced "*Metz cathedral is to let*". In 1802, after the Concordat, it was restored to the catholic cult.

In 1880, Notre-Dame portal which had been pulled down in 1766, was rebuilt. In 1903 the present-day neo-Gothic portal replaced on the west front the portal erected by Blondel in 1764.

The last war (1944) only damaged a few windows of lesser interest; when it replaced them, the Service des Monuments Historiques took care to enrich the cathedral's exceptional ensemble of stained-glass.

Excluding the restoration work carried out on the facades by the state. A significant project was inaugurated on the 17th of December 2006 by Mgr Pierre Raffin, bishop of Metz. The liturgical choir was modified, this work being entrusted to the architect in chief, Christophe Bottineau. Modern furnishings were designed by the artist, Mattia Bonetti. The "living stone" cathedral continues its perpetual mutation by the contribution of contemporary, creative projects following on from the cathedral builders.

Choir stalls: stall support "the grape-carriers".

The nave. ▶

INTERIOR

The **nave** is 42 metres high; this height combined with a rather narrow width (15m60 between the axes of the pillars) gives an impression of elevation and lightness. This feeling is increased by the fact that the side-aisles are relatively low, no more than 14m or one-third of the height of the nave.

Above the perforated triforium, a garland of leaves appears beneath a fold of supple drapery, perhaps recalling the tapestries and branches which decorated the church on feast-days. The lower part of the triforium is adorned by a frieze of trifoiled arcades ornamented with varied and original figurines and masks.

The vast area of windows, 6500 m2, lights the architectural ensemble and makes it one of the most luminous cathedrals in the world.

The first three bays are marked by four round pillars, 1m 64 in diameter*, very unseated at their base, which were part of the old collegiate church of Notre-Dame-la-Ronde.

The stained-glass windows on the north side are 15th Century.

To the right, open the choir stalls, and to the left, the back of the portal of Notre-Dame-La- Ronde.

On the reverse side of the grand portal are represented, on the lintel **(1)**: in the centre, the Virgin and child; on the right, the circumcision and the flight into Egypt, on the left, the Annunciation and the Visitation. At the end of the consoles are masks of the architect and the sculptor: Tornow (on the left) and Dujardin (on the right).

The **porphyry vat (12)**, sculpted in a monolithic block, on the right of the portal, comes from the ancient Roman baths. It was used as a baptismal font at the time when baptism was by immersion (length 2m92, height: 0m60).

In 1807, Monseigneur Jauffret succeeded in retaining it in the cathedral, when the town wished to offer it to Empress Josephine, wife of Napoleon Ist, as a decoration for the gardens of La Malmaison. Above, stained-glass window by Mayer of Munich (1905) **(12)**, Jesse's tree. On the right, Notre-Dame de Bon Secours, stone statue of the Virgin, (16th Century) **(13)**.

To the left of the statue is the epitaph of Master Hermann de Munster (in Westphalia) creator of the great rose-window of the west facade, who died on the 25th of March 1392 and is buried near his masterpiece.

On the right, epitaph of Colignon Cassamus of Metz, fiddler to king Alphonse de Castille of Spain and to Emperor Charles IV, who died in 1396.

Above, 13th Century windows **(13)**. Next to Christ and the Virgin, eight of the Messiah's ancestors, and eight apostles.

The mission cross, erected in 1825 **(14)** on Place Saint-Vincent, was transferred to the cathedral following the 1830 uprisings.

The stained-glass windows of the chancel of **Notre-Dame-la-Ronde** are by Mayer of Munich (1884) **(8)**. In the centre, the coronation of the Virgin; on the left, Saint Dominic receiving the Rosary; on the right, Simon Stock receiving the scapulary.

Notre-Dame-la-Ronde chapel, Virgin in glory, 19th C. stained-glass window (detail).

* the twelve other pillars measure 3m in diameter.

Notre-Dame-la-Ronde chapel,
Saint Clement, 19th C. window (detail).

The side-windows of the same origin (1904) represent the mysteries of the Rosary.

The altar designed by architect Racine (1859) is surmounted by a statue of the Virgin, a votive offering of the ladies of Metz. The railing dates from 1882.

Annunciation: 14th C. fresco.

At the entrance to the chapel, a bracket supports a series of carvings: on the left, a sow suckling two children while being given to drink in a bucket by a peasant; on the right, a little bearded personage astride a lion; beneath, an old man's head. These sculptures date from the 14th Century, the head having been restored in 1843.

On the wall to the left of the chapel, frescoes from the early 14th Century represent the Annunciation and the martyrdom of Saint Bartholomew. The rose-window above, from the 13th Century, represents the crowning of the Virgin.

On the left, a mobile pulpit, in Louis XV style (1728) **(15)**.

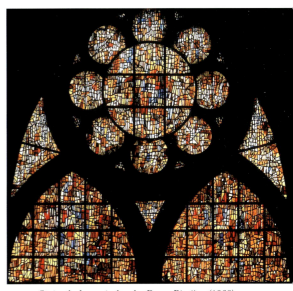

Stained-glass window by Roger Bissière (1960).

In the following bay, under the **portals of "la Mutte"** (south) and of the - **chapter** (north) in the tympana, stained-glass windows by Roger Bissiere (1960) **(16)**.

On the fourth south bay of the nave, at triforium level, an inscription in Gothic lettering, painted on joists, is a reminder of the organ which was backed opposite, at the chapter tower, until 1806. It was constructed in 1454 and had been modified several times.

In the following bays the stained-glass windows are by Gaudin (1959). They portray saints particularly honoured in the diocese of Metz (height 18m).

Chapel of the Blessed Sacrement: (10)

Begun in 1350, it was originally the funereal chapel of the bishops of Metz. Bishops Adémar de Monteil (1327-1361), Thierry Bayer de Boppard (1365-1384), Conrad Bayer de Boppard (1415-1459), Meurisse (suffragan 1629-1644) and Claude de Rouvroy de Saint-Simon (1733-1760) are all interred here.

Some fragments of epitaphs, discovered in 1858, helped in the restoration of the funereal inscriptions to be seen on the right and left of the chapel entrance. They concern bishops Adémar de Monteil and Thierry Bayer de Boppard.

The chapel windows were executed in 1957 **(10)** by Jacques Villon, whose real name was Gaston Duchamps, born in Damville (Eure) in 1875. He created these stained-glass windows at the age of 82. In the centre, the Crucifixion; on the left, the Last Supper; on the right, the wedding at Cana; in the side windows: on the left, the Jewish Passover; on the right, the rock at Mount Horeb.

To the left of the altar, Christ bound, 16th

Chapel of the Blessed sacrament: Christ bound, 16th C.

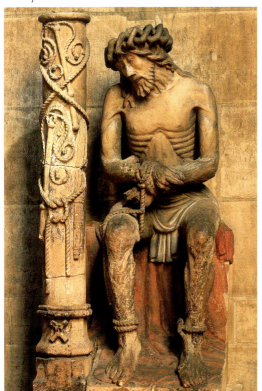

Century; the 18th Century railing decorated with leaves was forged by a pupil of the workshop of Jean Lamour, creator of the famous railings of the Place Stanislas in Nancy.

The wall frescoes of the pillars were restored by painter Bardenhewer of Cologne in 1909.

Facing the Blessed Sacrement chapel, in the fifth bay of the northern side-aisle, is a wooden statue of Saint Peter, whose altar was abolished in 1911.

Underneath, a commemorative plaque recalls the visit of Pope John-Paul II to Metz cathedral on the 10th of October 1988.

Engraved on the column of the righthand pilaster, the epitaph of canon Henri de Frontigny, who died on the 30th of November 1404.

Here also can be seen the tomb of Pierre Perrat **(17)**, architect of the cathedral

---

THE LEGEND OF PIERRE PERRAT

Pierre Perrat, the architect of Metz cathedral, was absorbed in the study of his plans, when suddenly appeared before him a little man who, in a few strokes, drew the plan of the cathedral and immediately wiped it out.

Pierre Perrat, in disbelief, begged his interlocutor to help him. The stranger then presented a parchment which Pierre Perrat signed unread. From that moment on, the architect had not the slightest difficulty in building his cathedral.

When he died he was put in a coffin sealed to a wall inside the cathedral.

*Some time later, the stranger presented himself with his parchment, claiming the body. Archangel Saint Michael, who was keeping watch, said to him: "**For you to take possession of the architect's soul, he must be buried; but as you see, his tomb is sealed in the wall**". The rueful stranger disappeared in a strong odour of sulphur. There can be no doubt that this being was none other than the Devil.*

(†1400) whose epitaph was reconstituted in error on the left of the door to the lower sacristy **(23)**.

In the southern side-aisle, an altar dedicated to Saint Claire, 16th Century wooden statue **(18)**.

◀ Chapel of the Blessed sacrament.

The ornamentation is inspired by 16th Century Flemish tapestries. Their interior is mostly red, the celestial symbol. It was based on wall-paintings in the cathedral, and realised in false relief in harmony with the case sculpture. (Created by Guy Vetter 1981).

16th C. suspended semi-circular organ (detail).

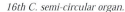

16th C. semi-circular organ.

(19) The great pulpit (1820) was created by two local artists: Francois Soret and Louis Daga. In 1837, Henri Lacordaire, a Dominican who reestablished the order of preaching brothers in France, preached the sermon of Advent from the pulpit, and in 1838 that of Lent.

Facing the pulpit, on the sixth southern pillar, a Christ in bronze (1861) (20), made by the parisian sculptor Duret (1804-1865).

The little semi-circular Renaissance organ (21) perched on the triforium of the eighth bay, was designed by Jean de Trèves (1537); the case, magnificently sculpted in Henri II style, was created by Jean de Verdun (1537). Since its latest restoration in 1981 by organmaker Marc Garnier, the instrument has nine sets of pipes.

Apart from improving the acoustics when they are open and protecting from the dust when closed, the shutters decorate the instrument. Their exterior is predominantly green, the earth symbol.

Saint Paul and saint Stephen. 13th C. window.

In the last bay of the southern side-aisle, on the wall, a statue of Saint Barbe (15th Century) **(22)**, donated in 1935 by Marie du Coëtlosquet.

Above, three 13th Century rose-windows **(22)**. In the centre, Saint Stephen and Saint Paul; on the left, the stoning of Saint Stephen; on the right, the martyrdom of Saint Bartholomew.

16th C. Rhenish art virgin.

Virgin and child: wall painting.

To the right of the door to the lower sacristy (1775), a 16th Century Virgin **(23)**, donated in 1908, is set on the emplacement of a 15th Century altar dedicated to Notre-Dame.

Above, two 13th Century rose-windows **(23)**. On the left, the Annunciation; on the right, the donator.

From the transept, let us admire the three greatest windows of the cathedral, on the **west**, **north** and **south** facades.

PLAN OF THE STAINED-GLASS WINDOWS OF THE WEST FRONT
Hermann de Munster (14th Century)

A - Christ.
B - Mary.
C - John.
D - Angels with a censer.
E - Angels.
F - Face of Christ.
G - St. Paul.
H - St. Stephen.
I - Musician angels.

1 - Philon.
2 - St. Bartholomew.
3 - David.
4 - St. Andrew.

5 - Isaiah.
6 - St. James
  the Less.
7 - Jonathan.
8 - St. Mathias.
9 - St. Stephen.
10 - St. Paul.
11 - St. Daniel.
12 - St. Simon.
13 - Jacob.
14 - St. James
  the Great.
15 - St. Joël.
16 - St. Philip.

14th C. stained-glass window by Hermann de Munster: the rose-window (detail).

*Musician angel . Hermann de Munster's window.
Detail of the great rose-window 14th C.*

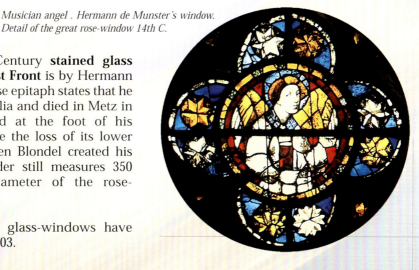

The 14th Century **stained glass window of the West Front** is by Hermann de Munster **(1)** whose epitaph states that he came from Westphalia and died in Metz in 1392. He is buried at the foot of his masterpiece. Despite the loss of its lower section in 1764 when Blondel created his portal, the remainder still measures 350 square metres (diameter of the rose-window: 11m25).

All stained glass-windows have been restaured in 2003.

PLAN OF THE STAINED-GLASS WINDOWS OF THE NORTH TRANSEPT
Thiébaut de Lyxheim (1504)

A - The coronation
   of the Virgin.
B - Angels and stars.

The evangelists
C - St. Luke.
D - St. Matthew.
E - St. Mark.
F - St. John.

1 - St. Anthony.
2 - St. Roch.
3 - St. Stephen.
4 - St. Blaise.
5 - St. Hubert.
6 - St. Michael.
7 - St. Cyriaque.

8 - St. Laurence.
9 - St. Agnes.
10 - St. Margaret.
11 - St. Barbe.
12 - St. Elizabeth.
13 - St. Apolline.
14 - St. Odile.
15 - St. Catherine.
16 - St. Madeleine.
17 - St. Paul.
18 - St. Matthew.
19 - St. Bartholomew.
20 - St. Philip.
21 - St. James.
22 - St. Thomas.
23 - St. Andrew.
24 - St. Peter.

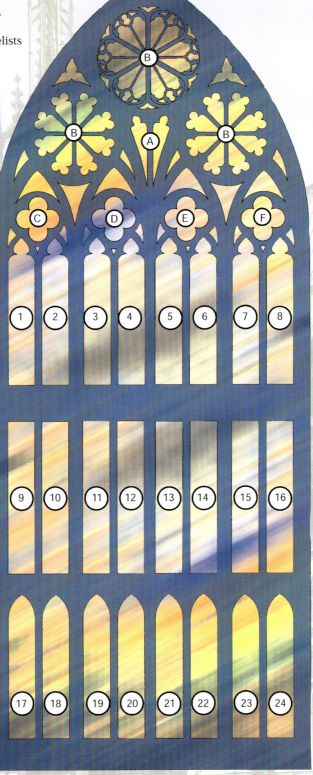

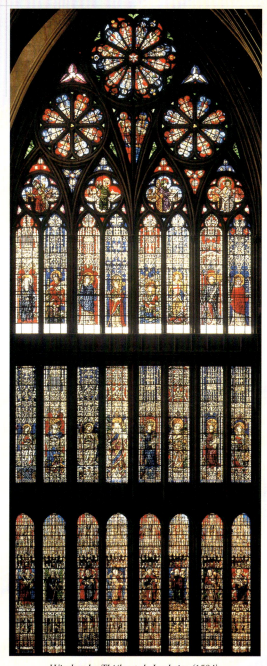

Window by Thiébaut de Lyxheim (1504).

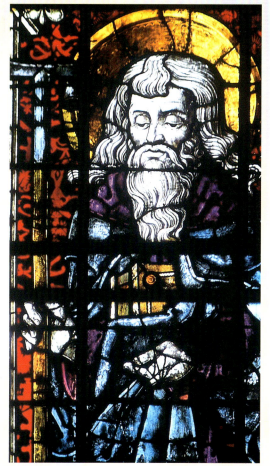

*Window by Thiébaut de Lyxheim:
Saint Anthony (detail).*

*Window by Thiébaut de Lyxheim:
The martyrdom of Saint Bartholomew (detail).*

The North Transept window, created in 1504, is due in part to Thiébaut de Lyxheim **(24)**. The ensemble portrays the triumph of the Virgin in Paradise. Although created in the 16th Century, the lower section is no longer the work of Thiébaut de Lyxheim, but probably of Thomas de Clinchamp. The window measures 424 square metres.

PLAN OF THE STAINED-GLASS WINDOWS OF THE SOUTH TRANSEPT
Valentin Bousch (16th Century)

A - Head of Christ.
B - Angels.
C - Chapter coat of arms.
D - Date MDXXI.
E - Date 1521.
F - St. Gregory.
G - St. Jerome.
H - St. Augustine.
I - St. Ambrose.
Ʋ - Monograms
of Valentin Bousch.

1 - St. Clement.
2 - St. Felix.
3 - St. Arnoul.
4 - St. Goëri.
5 - St. Auctor.
6 - St. Terence.

7 - St. Patient.
8 - Otto Savin.
9 - St. Barbe.
10 - St. Catherine.
11 - St. Mary and Jesus.
12 - St. Anne.
13 - St. Madeleine.
14 - St. Helen.
15 - St. Apolline.
16 - St. Margaret.
17 - St. Céleste.
18 - St. Siméon.
19 - St. Firmin.
20 - St. Legonce.
21 - St. Rufe.
22 - St. Adelphe.
23 - St. Urbice.
24 - Evrard Marlier.

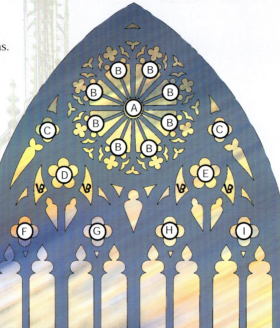

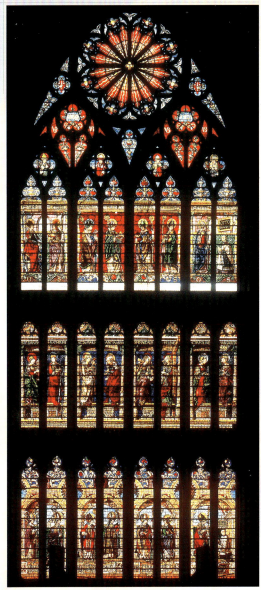

Window by Valentin Bousch 16th C.:
Saint Arnoul (detail).

Window by Valentin Bousch 16th C.:
Saint Apolline holding her tooth (detail).

The window of the South Transept by Valentin Bousch **(27)** is a perfect testimony of the change in style between the north and south facades of the transept. Barely twenty years separate the creation of these two windows; here the Renaissance masterpiece of italian inspiration is a total break away from the medieval style. It took six years of work to complete this stained-glass window, from 1521 to 1527. The personages dominate by their tall and imposing stature, framed by rich architecture. A rose-window of resplendent colour crowns the composition.

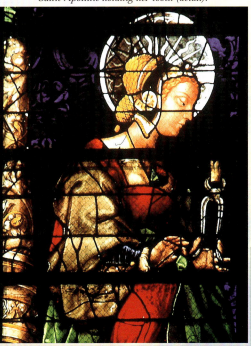

23

*Nativity. Sculpture of N-D de Lourdes chapel.
20th Century (detail).*

In the arm of the north transept, **the canopied altar (25)** was installed in 1911 in honour of Notre-Dame-de-Lourdes*

To the right of the altar, a tomb-statue of Jean de Heu, bishop of Toul in 1363, who died at Metz in 1372.

Above the altar's canopy, 15th Century stained-glass windows **(25)** portray scenes of the life of the Virgin. The base of these windows was amputated during the building of the upper sacristy in 1518. Above, windows by Marc Chagall (1970) **(25)** portray floral bouquets.

The great windows above date from 1501.

Those facing the altar **(26)** are from the beginning of the 16th Century. Below, a 1963 stained-glass window by Marc Chagall **(26)**: from left to right the creation of Adam and Eve, the Garden of Eden, the original sin, Adam and Eve driven out of Paradise.

At the base of the same wall, engraved in letters of gold on black marble, the epitaph of Charlotte-Eugénie de Choiseul-Stainville, last abbess of the Royal chapter of Saint-Louis in Metz.

Below Thiébaut de Lyxheim's window **(24)** the epitaph, reconstituted in 1981, of Bertram, bishop of Metz (1180-1212). Next to it, the epitaphs of canons Jean, Mathias and Francois Belchamps, installed in 1934 by members of their family.

*Chagall stained-glass window (1963):
the original sin.*

* There was already in 1245 in the cathedral's left transept a Notre-Dame chapel for Metz's German colony, hence its name: Notre-Dame-la-Tierce (the Teutsche).

The accompaniment organ in the south arm of the transept made by Haerpfer-Erman de Boulay in 1970 **(27)**, has 27 sets of pipes; the case was designed by architect Renard.

To the left of the organ are the cathedral's oldest stained-glass windows, dating from the early 13th Century **(28)**.

Saint Paul preaching, 13th C. window (detail).

They represent scenes from the life of Saint Paul. These windows probably come from Saint Paul's church, which was a part of the "*cathedral group*" pulled down in the 18th Century.

Above, 16th Century windows by Valentin Bousch **(28)**. Opposite, to the right of the organ, recomposition of windows installed in 1845 and 1864.

The great windows of the chancel are of the 16th Century, created by Valentin Bousch who completed them in 1539 **(30-36)**. The three windows of the apse were made from 1520 to 1523 at the Dukes of Lorraine's expense, under the control of their agent, canon Piguet (his chalice can be seen in the treasure-house).

In the centre, the stoning of Saint Stephen; on his right, cardinal Jean IV of Lorraine. In the left-hand window are portrayed the cardinal's parents, under the protection of their patron saints: his father Rene II who died in 1508 and his mother

Phillippe de Gueldre, who entered the convent of the order of Saint Claire at Pont-a-Mousson after the death of her husband. In the right-hand window: the cardinal's brother, duke Antoine and his wife duchess Renée de Bourbon.

The four other great chancel windows are also by Valentin Bousch. The small windows of the triforium were made from 1842 to 1845 by Laurent-Charles Maréchal and Joseph Cugnon, both from Metz: they portray holy bishops of Metz.

Window by Valentin Bousch 16th C.:
Duchess Renée de Bourbon (detail).

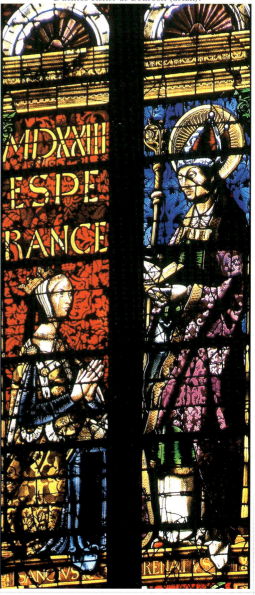

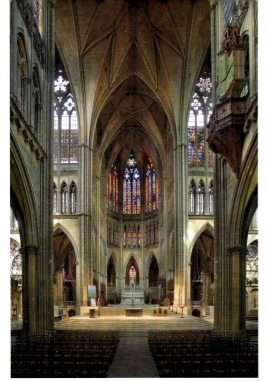

The choir.

At the entrance to the choir, the **ancient throne of Saint Clement (29)** throne of the bishops of Metz since Merovingian times, is carved in a column of cipolin marble of the Roman period.

Episcopal seat: Roman period.

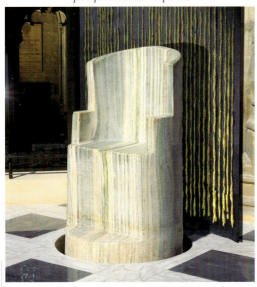

It integrates itself perfectly into the project initiated at the request of the Bishop of Metz, Mgr Pierre Raffin. The services of the state, in tight collaboration with the chapter of the cathedral and the work of the cathedral have entrusted the architect in chief, C. Bottineau the general outline of the renovation of the choir stalls. The task of

realising of the liturgical furnishings will be left to the Swiss artistic designer, Mattia Bonetti, who best corresponded to the liturgical programme affirming the presence of the altar, the ambo and the Episcopal seat. Bronze and marble were chosen as the materials chosen for the realisation of the new liturgical furnishings.

The bronze comes from the barrels of cannons bought for the work of the cathedral at the beginning of the 20th century.

The creation and installation of the liturgical furnishings were inaugurated and consecrated on the 17th of December 2006 by the bishop of Metz.

The choir-stalls **(34-36)** were created in the workshops of Theophile Klem at Colmar in 1913-1914 and definitely set up in 1922.

The marble high altar was sculpted by Petitmangin from designs by architect Racine (1865).

The enclosure of the choir, which separates it from the ambulatory, dates only from 1912; it was created by architect Schmitz.

Access to the ambulatory is by the north staircase; the balustrade and the railing were made by Tornow in 1882.

To the left, at the top of the stairs, a marble bust of Jacques-Benigne Bossuet **(37)**, cathedral canon from 1641 to 1669. Copy of the work by Coysevox, set up in 1921.

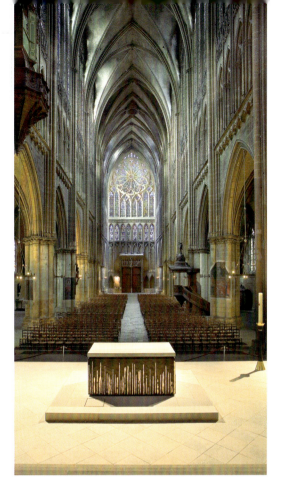

The ambulatory. ▶

Saint-Joseph Chapel (39)

It was given this name when the altar was consecrated in honour of this saint in 1867. In the vaulting keystone, the coat of arms of the Chapter. The windows are 16th Century, on the right: the Annunciation (1524), the two other windows come from Saint-Barbe's church and were placed in the cathedral in 1842.

Chapel of the Apse (40)

In the vaulting, the arms and name of cardinal Jean IV de Lorraine.

The middle window (1522) depicts, on the left, Saint Stephen, on the right, Saint Paul. The other two windows, 19th Century, are by Maréchal. They portray two bishops of Metz with their patron saint.

The altar dedicated to the Holy Virgin is decorated with a triptych from the Weis de Niederlahnstein workshops (1911).

On the left, the funeral monument of cardinal Anne d'Escars de Givry, born in

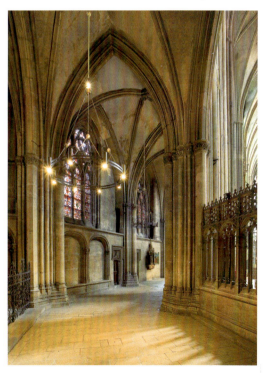

The first door leads to the upper sacristy which contains the treasure (description on page 32); To the right, a small door in flamboyant style with Renaissance leaves, leads to the turret of the golden globe.

The stained-glass windows above the doors are by Marc Chagall (37-38) French painter, engraver and decorator of Russian origin born at Vitebsk in 1887 who died at Saint-Paul-de-Vence in 1985. They were executed in 1960 and portray, from left to right: Abraham's sacrifice, Jacob's fight with the angel, Jacob's dream, Moses and the burning bush, Moses receiving the tables of the Law, David playing the harp, the crossing of the Red Sea, Jeremiah.

All Chagall's windows, like those of Villon and Bissière, were made in the workshop of Jacques Simon of Rheims by Charles Marq.

Paris in 1546, who took the habit of a Benedictine monk at the age of 8 years old, at Saint-Begnigne in Dijon. Bishop of Metz from 1608 to 1612, he died at Vic-sur-Seille, and was buried in Metz cathedral.

Saint-Livier Chapel (41)

Has been known by this name since 1868. The central keystone of the vaulting portrays the coat of arms of the chapter, the others the monograms of Jesus and Mary. The windows are 16th Century. The left one depicts a young unidentified saint dressed as a wealthy lord; the two other windows, installed in 1856, come from Sainte-Barbe's church.

Before the altar stand two tombs: one of Mgr. Dupont-des-Loges, bishop of Metz from 1842 to 1886, with on his right that of Mgr Fleck, bishop of Metz from 1886 to 1899.

The marble plaque on the left wall was placed there in 1906 in memory of Mgr d'Aubusson de la Feuillade, bishop of Metz from 1668 to 1697.

To the right of the altar, the funeral monument of Mgr Dupont-des-Loges, sculpted by Emmanuel Hannaux of Metz, inaugurated in 1923.

Ambulatory door, 15th C.

On the right, two doors in Renaissance style; the first **(42)** leads to the Charlemagne turret; the second **(43)** to a 16th Century vaulted sacristy.

The stained-glass windows above these two doors were made by Schmitz-Reuters of Aix-la-Chapelle (1882). On the left, the Church Fathers; on the right, Christ's ancestors.

To the right of the second door, a triptych **(43)** in neo-Gothic style, portrays in the centre Saint Clement holding enchained the "*Graoully*" dragon, on the left Saint Claire, on the right Saint Francis of Assisi. The inner and outer surfaces of the shutters depict scenes in the life of Saint Claire.

THE CRYPT (45)

Leaving the ambulatory, the access to the south crypt is on the right.

The present-day crypt was built at the same period as the choir (16th Century) which it supports.

In the Romanesque church, the crypt was smaller and had three chapels. Until 1780 the northern part was used to deposit the cathedral archives. The southern part which, following the demolition of the cloister in 1754, was used as the library, by 1777 housed the tombs of the canons and church employees. During the Revolution the two entrances to the crypt on the right and left of the choir were sealed, access being by the rue du Vivier.

Different parts of it were let for rent or used as cellars by the owners of houses backing onto the cathedral. The crypt was entirely restored between 1889 and 1900. The paving dates from this period. Stalls were set up in the north side of the chapel where even now the capitulary service is celebrated on weekdays during the winter.

At the entrance to the **first room**, on the right, is a model of the "*cathedral group*" before it was pulled down in 1754.

The pre-Romanesque crypt. ➤

The Graoully.
15th C. wooden head.

On the left, against the wall, an 18th Century painting depicts Saint Clement smiting the Graoully, which is suspended from the vault at the entrance to the second room (a reproduction made in 1864, but the wooden head is 15th Century).

Under the Graoully, fragments of a chancel, remains of a restoration made by Saint Chrodegang (742-766). The fragments were found in 1914, in the cathedral choir.

In **the second room** on the left, an entombment (16th Century) comes from the church of Xivry-Circourt (Meurthe-et-Moselle). It was brought to the cathedral in 1841 and restored by architect Schmitz in the early 20th Century.

Opposite, an ensemble of statuary from the diocesan museum includes a 15th Century multi-coloured Virgin, and an 11th Century baptistery.

Saint Blaise. 15th C. stone.

A saint. 15th C. wood

Saint John the Baptist. Wood.

Virgin. 15th C. coloured wood.

In the **third room**, copy of the equestrian statuette of Charlemagne, kept at the Louvre*.

Before the 18th Century, the original was the cathedral's property, together with another equestrian statuette of the same emperor in silver gilt which disappeared during the Revolution.

It is possible that the original dates from the caroligian epoch and is a portrait of Charlemagne made during his lifetime. The copy depicts the emperor on horseback, cloaked and crowned; in his hands were the orb and sword which no longer exist today.

In this room are also sacred objects and vases from the 13th to the 19th Centuries

In **the fourth room**, under the main choir, are vestiges of the 11th Century pre-Romanesque crypt:

The first right-hand pillar is reversed, the capital having become the base; remains of a Romanesque window. The central vault was reinforced in the 16th Century.

At the base of the carolingian (9th Century) altar, tombs of six bishops of Metz: Cardinal de Montmorency-Laval (1761-1802), who died in 1808 at Altona. (His remains were brought to Metz cathedral on the 4th of July 1900); Mgr Jauffret (1807-1823); Mgr Besson (1824-1842); Mgr Pelt (1919-1937); Mgr Heintz (1938-1958) and Mgr Schmitt (1958-1987). On the left against the wall, epitaph of Mgr Benzler, bishop of Metz from 1901 to 1919, buried in the abbatial church of Maria Laach in Germany.

The epitaphs on the right-hand wall refer to canons buried in the crypt: Jean Woirhaye (1825), Jacques Nicolas (1828), Gabriel Simon (1851) Ferdinand Flosse (1853) and Julien Laserre (1855).

Before leaving the pre-Romanesque crypt, let us pause for a moment before the last fragment of the tympanum of the 13th Century portal of the Virgin, pulled down in the 18th Century.

THE TREASURY (37)

A door dating from 1765 gives access to the treasury. This little vaulted room, built in around 1518, was the only sacristy of the choir. On the right, two wardrobes armoured with iron and 16th Century locks were at one time used to keep a part of the treasure.

This sacristy having been considered too small, the chapter had the big sacristy built in the 18th Century. Its walls are decorated with magnificent oak woodwork

Equestrian statue of Charlemagne (copy).

* *Bronze copy, made in 1882.*

Jacques-Bénigne BOSSUET

Born in Dijon in 1627.
Ecclesiastic and author.
Ordained priest in 1652, he was
archdeacon of Metz cathedral
from 1653 to 1659,
where he preached
his second funeral oration
at the death of
Henri de Gournay in 1658.
His sermons and orations were
monuments of pulpit eloquence; in
splendid language, inspired by the
reading of holy books, he drew from
them, as he put it, "*the great and terrible
lessons*" given by God to kings and
men. He was bishop of Condom, then of
Meaux. He died in Paris in 1704.

The Bawler. 15th C.

Facing the entrance, attached to the wall, the only vestige of the ancient great organ, suppressed in 1806: a 15th Century head, sculpted in oak, called "*the Bawler*", which opened and closed its mouth when the organist pulled the "*human voice*" stop.

The oldest item preserved in the treasury is **Saint Arnoul's ring** (he was bishop of Metz from 614 to 629 and died in 641). In solid gold, it bears, set on its bezel, an agate of milky cornaline engraved with a basket wherein a fish is caught and

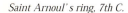

Saint Arnoul's ring, 7th C.

in Louis XV style. On the right, a painting of Christ crucified with Mary-Magdalen at his feet. An unsigned copy of the original work by Charles Monet, received by the chapter in 1765, damaged during the Revolution. On the left, above the door, a picture offered by Monseigneur Jauffret: the presentation of Jesus at the Temple, by an unknown artist, dating probably from 1765.

towards which two little fish are swimming (symbol of Christ and his faithful who are born to the grace of life in the water of baptism). Saint Arnoul, an ancestor of Charlemagne, is said, according to legend, to have found in the entrails of a fish served at table, the ring thrown into the Moselle before his bishopric.

13th C. enamelled reliquary (detail).

Enamelled reliquary of the second half of the 13th Century, from Limoges, in copper and ornamented by gilded copper and foliage, topped by a lid in the form of a roof. The sides are decorated by figures of angels. Saved in about 1793 from the profaned church of Saint-Eucaire of Metz, this precious object later became the property of Marie du Coëtlosquet, who donated it to the cathedral in 1923.

13th Century **altar stone** in agate, enshrined in a wooden frame, set in a silver mount. The underneath is decorated with lozenges enclosing flowers on an engraved base, the sides ornamented with gilded garlands of hammered leaves and curious birds with human heads; the top is surrounded on three sides by a band of inset silver; in the medallions are portrayed Christ as doctor and the attributes of evangelists Saint Matthew and Saint John.

In flamboyant Gothic style silver-gilt, the magnificent monstrance was presented on the occasion of the 18th international eucharistical congress held in Metz in 1907.

10th Century **crozier**, in ivory. Above the knot, this Romanesque crozier bears, on a setting of gilded copper, the names and symbols of the four rivers of Paradise: Tigris, Pishon, Gehon and Euphrates. Placed in the treasury in about 1835, this crozier belonged to Gorze abbey.

13th Century **ivory crozier**, attributed to bishop Renaud de Bar who donated it to the cathedral on the day of his enthronement in 1302, it is ornamented by a kneeling angel on the crozier knot, supporting a volute decorated with leaves in the centre of which, finely sculpted, on one side Christ crucified, between the Virgin and Saint John; on the other side the Virgin and Child between two angels.

13th C. ivory crozier (detail of the volute).

Lantern of the Great Precentor: replica of the ancient "*staff of the great precentor*", in use before the Revolution, melted down at the Mint during that period. The statuette of Saint Stephen, made in about 1802, could be 16th Century.

Statue of the Virgin bearing the Child-Jesus, created with Monseigneur Besson's silver plate. It is carried in procession on Assumption Day, the 15th of August.

Pope Pius VI's slipper offered to the famous Metz surgeon Antoine Louis whom the Pope (1775-1799) had consulted in 1789. Antoine Louis' niece bequeathed the precious souvenir to doctor Morlane, the founder of Metz maternity hospital, whose heirs donated it to the cathedral chapter.

17th Century **ivory crucifix**, offered by Monseigneur Besson, which is used at the Good Friday service. In the medallions are relics of the true cross and of various instruments of the Passion.

As well as its many rare examples of the **goldsmith's art**, the cathedral treasury possesses a fabulous collection of vestments.

Made by the Carmelite nuns of Metz, two complete sets of **vestments**: chasuble, dalmatica, tunic and their accessories, some called "*summer Carmelites*" (18th Century) others "*winter Carmelites*" (17th Century). They depict scenes from the life of Saint Teresa of Avila.

Carmelite ornament (detail).

The so-called Charlemagne cope is without doubt the most important item belonging to the cathedral treasury.

Wrongfully attributed to Charlemagne, this Byzantine cope is probably of the 12th Century. It is said to have been taken from the emperor of Constantinople's robingroom by the Crusaders. On a background of purple silk, great eagles are embroidered in gold thread, two superimposed in the centre and one at each extremity, wings

The so-called Charlemagne cope.

unfurled, with their heads in profile. Dragons seem to be biting their feet, and the foliage that separates them ends in snakes' heads. At a later date, a hood picturing the crucifixion of Our Lord was attached to it. In the 16th Century, in order to consolidate the cope, two ornamental ofrays were added to it, depicting on the left three angels in a Renaissance frame bearing, from bottom to top: the holy tunic, the cross, the crown of thorns and the whips of the flagellation; on the right, three angels bearing the flagellation pillar, a ladder and the three traditional nails.

Part of the treasure, including the socalled Charlemagne cope, was carried away by the German army during the 1944 debacle; the ensemble was later found in a Bavarian salt-mine and returned to Metz cathedral after the Liberation in 1945 by American general Patton.

After the Revolution little remained of the cathedral's ancient treasure, enriched during the centuries by donations from illustrious personages such as Charlemagne, Charles le Chauve and bishops and canons.

Already in the 16th Century many jewels were sacrificed to help pay for the cost of wars waged by the great of this world; in the 17th precious manuscripts such as Charles le Chauve's psalter and bible were "*offered*" to Colbert. Under the Revolution the treasure's dispersion was complete.

Martin Pinguet chalice. 15th C.

During the 19th Century the cathedral chapter endeavoured to reconstitute it, in particular thanks to important donations by the bishops who succeeded one another on Saint Clement's throne.

Pontifical chapel:
(Dupont Des Loges) 19th C.

EXTERIOR

The plan bears witness to the two churches, Saint Etienne cathedral and Notre-Dame collegiate church, originally separated by an interior wall, then united after the completion of the upper nave. Consequently the cathedral's two towers were not on the west front, but only at the fourth bay.

Despite the length of time taken for the construction, from the 13th to the 16th Centuries, the edifice has a remarkable unity of style. This harmony was disturbed by some 18th Century additions (since disappeared) also of the 19th and 20th Centuries during the construction of the great portal.

Portal of the Virgin (6)

This portal dates from the second half of the 13th Century; blocked by Blondel during the building of his arcades, it was cleared in 1868. Rebuilt in 1880 by German architect Paul Tornow and French sculptor Louis Dujardin, it was inaugurated at Easter 1885 by Mgr Dupont-des-Loges.

Some sculptures of the ancient 13th Century portal were saved: the meeting of the Apostles, the dormition (death-like sleep until the Assumption) of the Virgin, the crowning of the Virgin (partly restored in the 19th Century) and the 13th Century crucifixion, one of the portal's most interesting scenes.

OUTLINE OF THE PORTAL OF THE VIRGIN

A - Virgin
B - Capital sins
C - Musician angels
D - An ancestor of Christ
E - Angels
F - Old people from the Apocalypse
G - The Prophets
H - The pagan prophetesses
I - The Last Judgement
K - The Resurrection
L - The Ascension
M - Crucifixion

N - The flagellation.
O - The carrying of the cross.
1 - St. Anne.

2 - St. John the Baptist.
3 - St. Cecilia.
4 - St. Stephen.
5 - St. Helen.

6 - St. Gregory.
7 - St. Clement.
8 - The Church.
9 - St. Mark.
10 - St. Matthew.
11 - St. Joachim.
12 - St. Joseph.
13 - St. Lucy.
14 - St. Laurence.
15 - St. Monica.
16 - St. Jerome.
17 - St. Arnoul.
18 - The Synagogue.
19 - St. Luke.
20 - St. John.

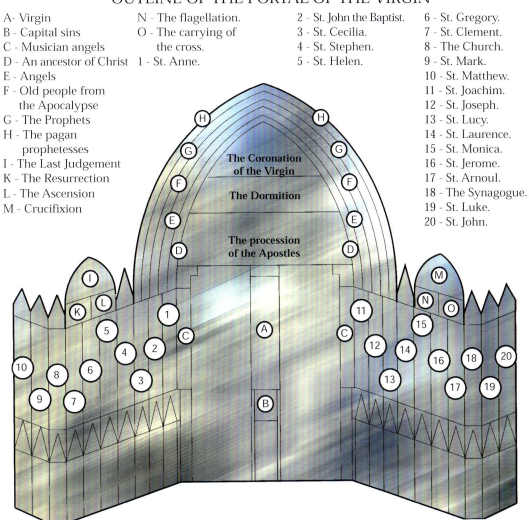

The Coronation of the Virgin

The Dormition

The procession of the Apostles

The central pier bears the main figure: The "*Smiling Virgin*".

The five-sided plinth of the pier evokes the seven capital sins (from left to right): cowardice, conceit, pride, superstition, meanness, lust and despair.

The embrasures of the two entrances bear six figures depicting rows of choirs of angels with their musical instruments; they end on four corbels ornamented with leaves and figurines holding up the lintel. On the left, Jacob fighting the angel; on the right, the victory of man over the dragon. The sculptures of the pier portray two angels. To the left of the pier: large statues depicting Saint Anne, Saint John the Baptist, Saint Cecilia, Saint Stephen, Saint Helen, Saint Gregory the Great, Saint Clement, the Church, two evangelists, Saint Mark and Saint Matthew. To the right of the pier: Saint Joachim, Saint Joseph, Saint Lucy, Saint Laurence, Saint Monica, Saint Jerome, Saint Arnoul, the Synagogue, two evangelists: Saint Luke and Saint John.

*Portal of the Virgin: the dragon
(detail of a chamfer).*

In its lower section, below the big statues, rows of triangular chamfers. To the left of the pier: a lily in the shadow of a crown; an angel holding a sun; two cardinal virtues, temperance mixing hot and cold liquid, justice blindfold; the pelican, symbol of Christ's sacrifice; the phoenix, symbol of the Resurrection; the eagle, figure of

regeneration by water and the Spirit; the lion, symbol of Christ; the four rivers of Paradise: Euphrates, Tigris, Gihon, Pishon, followed by two symbols of the evangelists: the lion and man, finally the tree of life.

To the right of the pier: a lily; an angel holding a half-moon, two cardinal

*Portal of the Virgin: the elephant
(detail of a chamfer).*

virtues: strength holding a sword, prudence holding a serpent; the symbols of the four elements: the elephant, symbol of the earth, the dove symbol of the air, the whale symbol of water, the dragon symbol of fire; the four cardinal winds: Aeolia, Aurora, Zephyr, Boreas; followed by two symbols of the evangelists: the bull and the eagle; and finally the stricken tree.

The figures seated beneath canopies which ornament the two sides of the curved interior surface of the transversal arch depict: on the left, the Church, above, Abel carrying the lamb, the wise virgins and Christ in majesty; on the right, the Synagogue, above, Cain carrying a wheatsheaf, the foolish virgins and Satan, upside down, brandishing a whip. At the keystone, the symbol of Christ.

The two false side tympana portray: on the Church side, the Last Judgement; the Resurrection; the Ascension. On the Synagogue side: scenes of the Crucifixion (13th Century); the Flagellation, the carrying of the Cross.

Sculptures decorate the oblique sides of the intrados and frame the portal tympanum.

On each side, five rows of statues represent: the kings, ancestors of the Virgin and Jesus, angels, old people from the Apocalypse, prophets and patriarchs. Finally, on either side, the pagan prophetesses who announced the coming of the Saviour.

At the summit of the vault, a gathering of clouds, symbols of Heaven.

The portal tympanum evokes the dormition of the Virgin. Two apostles stand near the funereal couch: at the head, Saint John; at the foot, Saint Peter holding in his right hand a holy-water sprinkler that he is dipping in a font. In the centre, the Saviour appears, extending his right hand in blessing, while his left holds a figurine representing the Virgin's soul. On either side of the Saviour, angels emerge from the clouds; they are about to receive the Virgin's soul to carry it to Heaven, and as a sign of respect, their hands are veiled.

Next to Saint John and Saint Peter, two angels carry censers and incense bowls.

In the lower section: in the centre, two angels, the one on the right carrying the censer, the other (archangel Gabriel) carrying the lily branch and the font.

In the upper section: Christ crowns his mother. Two angels present crowns; the two personages at either end kneel in the attitude of prayer.

In the niches which surmount the portal's supporting pillars, a statue of Charlemagne on the left, and of Saint Louis on the right.

On the pediment, the latin inscription reads: " *You are beautiful, charming in your delights, holy mother of God*".

On leaving the portal of the Virgin, to the right is the octagonal turret of the clock.

As early as 1382, chronicles mention a clock on this tower. In 1504, as is indicated by the date over it, the dial was replaced. Below, the coat of arms of the town. The angel on the right, holding a sundial, was only added in 1903. There are three bells in the tower.

Let us now continue to **the cathedral square**, where the bishops' residence used to stand. Cardinal de Montmorency - Laval, bishop of Metz from 1761 to 1802 began the construction of a new palace which remained unfinished. Since 1831 its substructures have been used as a covered market . Recently repaved, the square presents today an interesting view of the ensemble of the west front which, until 1764, served only as a private passageway for the bishop, by a little door under the great window. In the 18 th Century, in order to give sufficient height to his Classic style portal, Blondel amputated the base of the great 14th Century stained-glass window (1764). In the early 20th Century, that portal was replaced by the present one, made by Tornow and Dujardin.

This new portal was inaugurated in 1903 in the presence of Emperor William II.

The great portal built by Blondel in the 18th Century (document from the archives).

OUTLINE OF THE GREAT PORTAL

A - Christ.
B - David.
C - Wise virgins.
D - Foolish virgins.
E - Cherubs.
F - Seraphs.
G - Dominations.
H - Numbers.
 I - Archangels.
K - Principalities.
L - Angels.
M - Sybils and prophets.

1 - St. Peter.
2 - St. Andrew.
3 - St. Thomas.

4 - St. Simon.
5 - St. Matthew.
6 - St. Philip.

7 - St. Stephen.
8 - Old Testament.
9 - St. Paul.
10 - St. John.
11 - St. James the Great.
12 - St. James the Less.
13 - St. Bartholomew.
14 - St. Jude.
15 - St. Paul.
16 - New Testament.

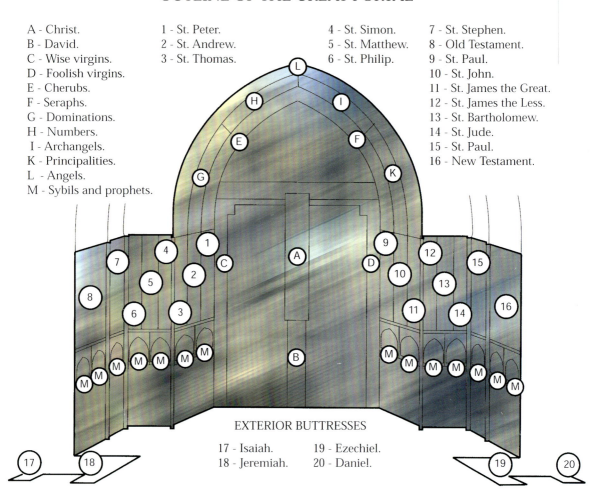

EXTERIOR BUTTRESSES

17 - Isaiah.
18 - Jeremiah.
19 - Ezechiel.
20 - Daniel.

Great portal (Christ portal) (1)

On the central pillar, Christ, the principal figure of the portal, stands on the lion and the dragon, blessing with his right hand and holding the Gospel in his left; in the niche below, King David.

To the left and right, backing on to columns, the twelve Apostles: all have beneath their feet their persecutors and in hand the instrument of their execution.

On the left of the portal:
-Saint Peter holding in his right hand the keys of Heaven, in his left hand a cross; at his feet, Simon the magician.
-Saint Andrew with the normal cross, at his feet proconsul Aegée d'Achaïe.

-Saint Thomas holding a hatchet, at his feet the king of India.
-Saint Simon with the sword, at his feet a pagan priest.
-Saint Matthew with the sword, at his feet King Hyrax.
-Saint Philip also with the sword, at his feet King Hieropolis.

On the right of the portal:
-Saint Paul, sword in hand, at his feet Emperor Nero.
-Saint John, young, beardless, with a tonsure, wearing the amict, the alb and the chasuble, holding in his hands a chalice with a snake, at his feet the highpriest of Diana presenting to him a cup filled with venom.

-Saint James the Great, holding the sword, wearing the scarf adorned with shells, at his feet King Herod.
-Saint James the Less, holding in his hand a long club, at his feet the fuller who gave him the blow.
-Saint Bartholomew with a cutlass and a book, at his feet the Indian king Astrages.
-Saint Jude Thaddaeus holding a book, at his feet a soldier.

On the casements, to the left, the wise virgins, below, the tree of life whose branches bear fonts; to the right, the foolish virgins, below, the stricken tree destined to be felled.

The lintel over the two leaves of the door is supported by four corbels decorated with angels holding crowns and censers.

The tympanum presents scenes of the Last Judgement and has three sections.

In the lower section, eight niches portray scenes of the resurrection of the dead.

In the middle section, the angel of the Last Judgement weighs the souls: the one on the left, depicted as a lamb, pushes down the scale; the one on the right, depicted as a horrible mask, cannot prevent the tray from rising. On either side an angel blows a trumpet to waken the dead. On the left, guided by an angel, the good are received by Saint Peter; on the right the damned, naked, are led by the Prince of Darkness and thrown into the flames of Hell. In the upper section Christ, judge of the world, showing his wounds, passes the sentence of judgement. By His side, the Virgin and Saint John, who raise their supplicating hands towards Him; two angels bear the instruments of the Passion; two others carry the sun and the moon.

This tympanum is framed on either side by three rows of archivolts with figures of nine choirs of angels.

The first contains, on the left, seven figures of cherubs; on the right the same number of seraphs.

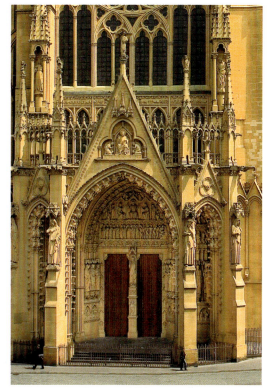

Great portal (Christ portal).

The second on the left, depicts in the four lower figures, the dominations; in those above, the same number of powers; while the row on the right represents, below, four principalities, above Archangels Michael, Gabriel, Raphael and Uriel.

In each of the exterior archivolts: to left and right, below, three angels blow trumpets; above, three angels carry candlesticks; finally, three angels carry censers.

The scenes of the Last Judgement are prolongated on either side of the portal in the lateral tympana.

On the left-hand side, Heaven: in the two lower sections, the souls of the chosen are borne by angels to the bosom of Abraham; in the upper section Abraham, on a throne, holds the souls of the chosen on his knees.

On the right-hand side, Hell: in the two lower sections, a group of damned led by the servants of the Prince of Darkness; in the upper section is Satan himself, seated on his throne with two demons by his side.

41

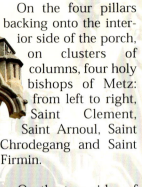

On the four pillars backing onto the interior side of the porch, on clusters of columns, four holy bishops of Metz: from left to right, Saint Clement, Saint Arnoul, Saint Chrodegang and Saint Firmin.

On the two sides of the porch: on the left, Saint Stephen, with Saul at his feet; on the right Saint Paul, with Nero at his feet. At either end are scenes of the martyrdom of these two saints.

On the left, from the exterior towards the interior: Saint Stephen preaching; his condemnation; the Jews laying aside their clothes before stoning him; above, the stoning of the saint.

On the right, from the interior towards the exterior: Saint Paul on the road to Damascus; Saint Paul preaching; Saint Paul refusing the people's sacrifices; above, the

The prophet Daniel.

Apostle's decapitation. Below, quadrifoils portray on the left scenes of the Old Testament and on the right, scenes from the New.

Under the great full-length statues: the sibyls and the lesser prophets.

The archivolts of the entrance's three openings are each decorated by two rows of figures seated under canopies depicting: martyrs, the virtues, confessors and the liberal arts.

In the middle archivolt aere portrayed: old people, kings of the Apocalypse and christian virgins.

In the keystone is the Lamb of God; the main coving is decorated with twelve medallions representing the signs of the Zodiac.

On the buttresses sustaining the outer part of the porch, the four great prophets: from left to right, Isaiah, Jeremiah, Ezechiel and Daniel; these buttresses are surmounted by the symbols of the four evangelists.

In the niche of the gable, Christ in triumph surrounded by angels kneeling in adoration and bearing censers.

The gable over the portal is terminated by archangel Saint Michael striking down the dragon. Under the canopies on either side of the great rose-window, two large statues: the Church and the Synagogue.

Notre-Dame-la-Ronde Portal (3)

The 13th Century bas-reliefs escaped destruction during the revolutionary period. An elegant drapery runs along each side.

On the right: scenes of the life of King David and Saint Helen; further along, scenes in the life of Saint Margaret and Saint Stephen.

On the left: figurines depicting fantastic personages and animals, similar to those of medieval bestiaries.

Saint-Etienne Portal (4)

On the central pillar, a statue of Saint Stephen by Metz sculptor Charles Pêtre (1866).

Above the doors, two bas-reliefs by Tornow and Dujardin (1896): the stoning of Saint Stephen and Saint Clement baptising.

Chapter tower (4)

The chapter tower (height 60m) is decorated on both sides with rich draperies sculpted in the 13th Century.

The upper part was built from 1840 to 1843. At mid-height is a monumental crucifix (5m20) made in 1894 by Dujardin; it replaces the great Christ destroyed in 1794. There are five bells in the tower.

To the right of the tower are three flying buttresses with monumental statues (height: 2m50). Right to left: Saint John the Apostle, Christ and Saint Thomas, and finally Saint Peter.

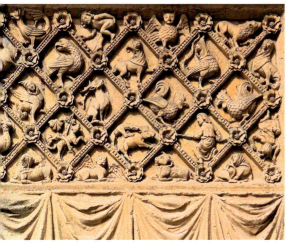

12th C. bestiary (detail).

Christ and Saint Thomas.

43

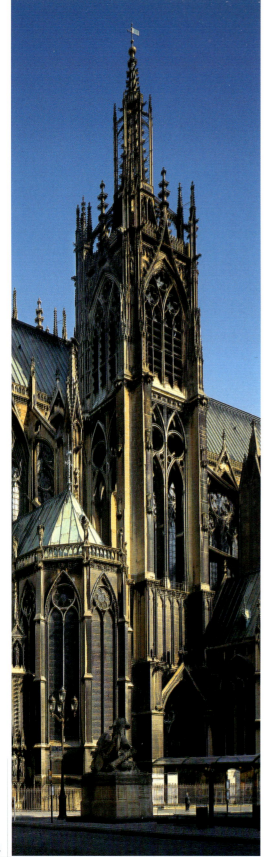

On the **northern façade** of the transept, the gable added in 1886 after construction in 1883 of a new roof is surmounted by a Virgin of 2m 40 in height.

Two polygonal towers flank the great choir: the tower of the Golden Globe **(11)** on the north side, which was originally crowned by a gilded copper ball, now replaced by a floral ornament; the tower of Charlemagne, on the south side **(11)**.

On the **south facade of the transept**, at the summit of the pointed arch of the great stained-glass window, statues of Saint Stephen, Saint Nicholas and Saint Goëri. The bas-reliefs depict the capital sins and also the bust of architect Tornow with a chisel in his hand.

Chapel of the Holy Sacrement (10)

Begun in the 14th Century, completed in 1443 in the flamboyant style by Jean de Commercy, it was seriously damaged by bombing during the Liberation of Metz in 1944.

Mutte Tower (9)

90 metres in height, the name is that of its big bell. The spire is a creation of architect Jean de Ranconval (1478-1481), replacing the old wooden steeple in which the bell had been suspended since 1381. It was

Mutte tower, "the Jester".

Mutte tower.

Metz cathedral: south side.

entirely reconstructed to the same designs as the old one in 1909 by architect Schmitz and restored from 1952 to 1960.

Since 1381, the Mutte bell has been recast some ten times, the last being in 1605. It weighs approximately 11 tons. Its height is 2m30, its diameter 2m32. Its peal rang out for the last time in 1918 during the Victory celebrations. Every day it chimes the twelve strokes of noon, and on election days every quarter hour.

There are two other bells in the tower: the Tocsin and "*Mademoiselle de Turmel*".

On the spire of the Mutte tower is a curious sculpture portraying a "*Jester*" covered in bells who seems to be crying out his distress to humanity.

The **apsis of Notre-Dame-la-Ronde collegiate church (8)** is the chancel of the old 13th Century collegiate church. On the wall, the Foch memorial is a memento of the Marshal's visit in 1918.

The buttresses which flank the apsis are crowned by two eagles. The pillar statues are of musicians.

The ancient gently sloping roof was destroyed by fire in 1877, due to a fireworks display in honour of the first visit by Emperor William 1st. It was replaced by a copper covering; the ridge being raised by 4m50.

After a violent hurricane in December 1952, it was necessary to replace the entire roof in copper sheeting (2000m2). To crown this work, the "*angel with a trumpet*", made of forged and gilded copper, was hoisted to the summit of the choir, 60 metres above ground-level, in 1959.

One cannot leave the cathedral without admiring once more this great edifice which, as the years go by, regains that golden yellow appearance reminiscent of the time of its builders. Like all the world's cathedrals, it is in a state of perpetual renaissance in the capable hands of the restorers. It lives by the faith and love of mankind which it transmits to God. Watch the sun reveal the warmth of this stone and do not leave before having paid your respects to Saint-Etienne at nightfall, before is extinguished this "**Lantern of God**", a great picture-book, eternal source of discovery and meditation.

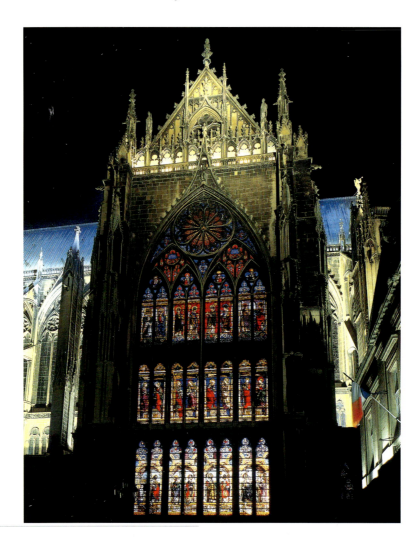

DIMENSIONS OF METZ CATHEDRAL
COMPARED WITH OTHER CATHEDRALS

TOTAL LENGTH . . . . 136 m
INTERIOR LENGTH 123 m20
Saint Peter's Vatican 186 m36
Saint Paul's London . . . . 158 m
Milan . . . . 148 m
Rheims 138 m70
Amiens 133 m50
Saint Paul outside the walls (Rome) . . 131 m
Chartres . . . . 130 m
Paris 127 m50
Bourges 117 m90
Strasbourg . . . . 110 m

LENGTH OF THE TRANSEPT . . . 46 m80
Saint Peter's Vatican . . . . 138 m
Milan . . . . 88 m
Amiens . . . . 70 m
Chartres 64 m50
Beauvais 58 m60
Rheims 49 m45
Paris . . . . 48 m
Strasbourg . . . . 41 m

WIDTH OF THE GREAT NAVE . . . 15 m60
Saint Peter's Vatican 27 m50
Milan . . . . 20 m
Chartres 16 m40
Strasbourg . . . . 16 m
Bourges 14 m93
Rheims 14 m65
Amiens 14 m60
Cologne 13 m80
Paris 12 m50
WIDTH OF THE TRANSEPT 16 m80

INTERIOR HEIGHT
Transept . . . . 43 m
High nave . . . . 42 m
Side naves 14 m30
Saint Peter's Vatican (dome) . . . 119 m
                    (nave) . . . . 44 m
Beauvais (choir) 48 m20
Milan (dome) 64 m60
        (nave) 46 m80
Cologne 43 m50

Amiens 42 m30
Rheims 37 m95
Bourges and Chartres . . . . 37 m
Paris 32 m50
Strasbourg . . . . 32 m

HEIGHT OF THE TOWERS
Mutte Tower . . . . 90 m
Chapter Tower . . . . 60 m
Ulm . . . . 161 m
Cologne . . . . 156 m
Strasbourg . . . . 142 m
Saint Peter's Vatican (dome) . . . 132 m50
Chartres . . . . 115 m
Amiens (spire) 112 m70
        (north tower) . . . . 66 m
Milan 108 m50
Rheims 81 m50
Paris . . . . 69 m
Bourges . . . . 66 m
TOTAL AREA OF THE
STAINED-GLASS WINDOWS . . . . 6.496 m²
Rouen . . . . 3.000 m²
Chartres . . . . 2.000 m²
Strasbourg . . . . 1.500 m²

TRANSEPT WINDOWS
(the biggest in the world)
33m25x12m75=424m² x2 . . . . 848 m²
WEST FRONT WINDOW . . . . . 349 m² 80
Strasbourg . . . . 200 m²
Bourges . . . . 150 m²

GREAT ROSE-WINDOW (diameter) . 11 m25
Strasbourg . . . . 14 m
Chartres 13 m36
Paris 9 m60

INTERIOR AREA . . . . 3.500 m²
Saint Peter's Vatican (dome) . . . . 15.160 m²
Milan . . . . 11.300 m²
Amiens . . . . 7.700 m²
Rheims (built area) . . . . 6.650 m²
Cologne . . . . 6.166 m²
Paris . . . . 5.955 m²
Strasbourg . . . . 4.087 m²

Window by Valentin Bousch 16th C.: Angels.

USEFUL INFORMATION

ASSOCIATION DES AMIS
DE LA CATHEDRALE DE METZ
DITE ŒUVRE DE LA CATHEDRALE
2, PLACE DE CHAMBRE
57000 METZ

MASSES
Sundays: 8h, 9h, 10h, 11h30.
Weekdays: 8h40 Masse 9h.

GUIDED TOURS
All the year around
for private visitors

school groups - adult groups
(from 12 persons upwards)

VISITS OF THE CRYPT AND THE TREASURY

INFORMATION - RESERVATION

Œuvre de la cathédrale de Metz
Guided visits service
2, place de chambre
57000 METZ
Tél. 03 87 75 54 61 - Fax 03 87 76 34 75
mail: contact@cathedrale-metz.fr
http://www.cathedrale-metz.fr

This document is not contractual,
the above times may be modified.

Exclusivité Œuvre de la cathédrale de Metz
All rights strictly reserved: no part of this publication may be reproduced
Photographs by **J.J.** & **A. Derenne**.
Layout **R. Roy** & **A. Derenne**.
Edition anglaise 2ème trimestre 2010 ISBN 2 - 904879 - 08 - 0